Contents

Ships 4

Carts and lorries 6

Coaches and buses 8

Bicycles 10

Trains 12

Cars 14

Aeroplanes 16

Spacecraft 18

Transport timeline 20

Glossary 22

Index 24

Ships

 850 **Viking longships**

Viking longships had one mast and one sail. The Vikings used oars to move their longships through the water.

 1620 **The Mayflower**

The Mayflower had three masts and lots of sails. The wind moved the ship through the water.

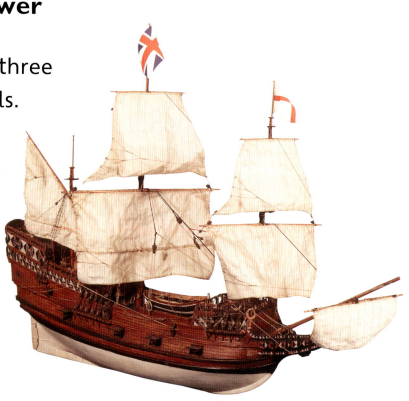

1858 The Great Eastern

The Great Eastern had a steam engine. It had sails, a propellor and two paddle wheels to move it through the water.

 ## present Ships now

Ships now have powerful diesel engines. Oil tankers are the biggest ships at sea.

Carts and lorries

 Animal power

Carts were pulled by horses and oxen.
Carts could carry people and goods.
They had one set of wheels.

 Traction engines and steam wagons

Traction engines and steam wagons had steam engines. They had two sets of wheels.

1930 **Diesel and petrol lorries**

Lorries had diesel or petrol engines. They could carry much more than steam wagons. Lorries had two sets of wheels.

 present **Lorries now**

Lorries now use diesel engines. They have many sets of wheels so they can carry very heavy loads.

Coaches and buses

 Stagecoach

Stagecoaches could carry six to eight people. Some passengers sat on the roof.

 Horse-drawn omnibus

Omnibuses carried up to 24 people. Passengers had to climb a ladder to get to the top deck. They had to sit on a bench.

London double decker bus

Double decker buses carried up to 60 people. They had stairs inside to get to the top deck.

 Buses now

Buses now come in all shapes and sizes. Some are double decker and some have only one deck.

Bicycles

 1816 **The Hobby Horse**

The Hobby Horse had no pedals or brakes. The riders had to push with their feet. It was a bumpy ride.

1880 **The Pennyfarthing**

The Pennyfarthing had pedals and brakes. The pedals made the front wheel go round. It was a dangerous ride.

The Safety Bicycle

The Safety Bicycle had pedals and brakes. The pedals made the back wheel go round by turning a chain. It had tyres filled with air. It was a smoother ride.

 Bicycles now

Bicycles or bikes now have pedals, brakes and gears. The gears help to make the bike go fast.

Trains

 The Rocket

The Rocket was one of the first trains. It had a steam engine. It moved very slowly.

 Steam trains

Steam trains were the first trains to cross America. They burnt wood to make steam.

1938   ## The Mallard

The Mallard had a better steam engine than the first trains. It burnt coal. It was a fast train. It could travel at over 100 miles an hour.

present   ## Trains now

Trains now use diesel or electricity to make the engine work. Some trains go very fast. The TGV in France can go at over 180 miles an hour.

Cars

 1861 **Steam cars**

Steam cars were very slow. A man had to keep filling the boiler to make the car run.

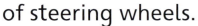 **1894** **Petrol cars**

The first petrol cars were also slow. They had chains to turn the wheels. They had levers instead of steering wheels.

1908 **Model 'T' Ford**

The Ford was the first car built in a factory. It had a steering wheel and good brakes.

 present **Cars now**

Cars now come in all shapes and sizes. They are comfortable and some can go very fast.

Aeroplanes

1903 — **The Flyer**

The Wright brothers made the first aeroplane with an engine. It could only carry the pilot. It was made of wood and cloth and had a small engine.

1930 — **DC-3**

The DC-3 was the first airliner and was made of metal. It had two powerful engines. It could carry many passengers.

1954 Boeing 707

The Boeing 707 was the first jet airliner in America. It had four big jet engines. It flew faster than other passenger airplanes.

 ## present Planes now

Planes now are bigger and faster. Jumbo jets can carry over 300 passengers. Concorde is the fastest passenger plane of all.

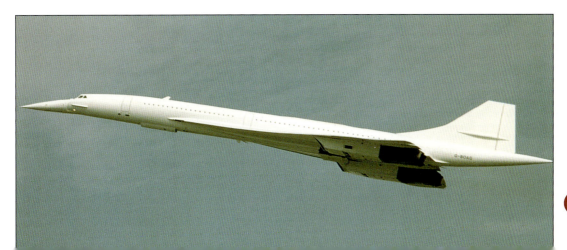

Spacecraft

 Sputnik

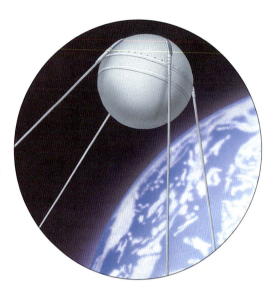

Sputnik was the first satellite in space to go round the Earth. It did not carry any people.

 Vostok 1

Vostok 1 was the first spacecraft to carry a person into space. His name was Yuri Gagarin.

1969 Apollo 11

Apollo 11 was the first spacecraft to land on the moon. Neil Armstrong and Buzz Aldrin were the first people to walk on the moon.

present Spacecraft now

Space shuttles carry people into space so they can visit or work at a space station. Each space shuttle can be used more than once.

Transport timeline

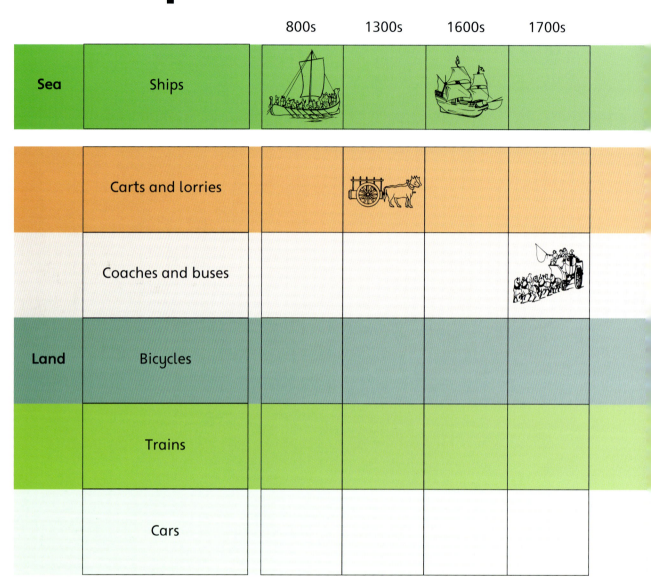

This timeline shows the main kinds of transport you can see in this book. It shows the progression from 800 to the present day. Look at each form of transport. When did air transport begin? What do you think transport in the future will be like?

	1800s	1900s	present

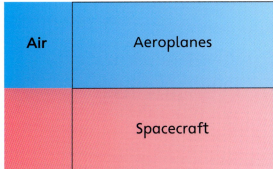
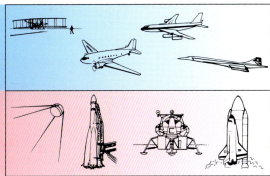

Air	Aeroplanes		
	Spacecraft		

boiler
a tank for making water hot or turning it into steam

brakes
the parts of a car, bicycle, lorry or train that help it to slow down

diesel engine
an engine that uses diesel to make it go

engine
the part of a car, lorry or train that makes it go. An engine works by burning diesel, petrol, wood or coal. It powers the wheels so that they go round.

gears
a set of special wheels (cogs) that work together to transfer the power from an engine to the wheels

mast
a tall pole that is used to hang the sails of a boat or ship

petrol engine
an engine that burns petrol to make it go

propeller
a set of blades that spin round very quickly to make a ship or plane move

satellite
an object that goes round the Earth in space

steam engine
an engine that burns wood or coal to make it go

traction engine
a steam or diesel engine which was used to pull very heavy loads

Index

Apollo 11 19

Boeing 707 17

carts 6
Concorde 17

DC-3 16
diesel lorries 7

Flyer, The 16

Great Eastern, The 5

Hobby Horse, The 10
horse-drawn omnibus 8

jumbo jets 17

London double decker bus 9

Mallard, The 13

Mayflower, The 4
Model 'T' Ford 15

oil tankers 5

Pennyfarthing, The 10
petrol cars 14

Rocket, The 12

Safety Bicycle, The 11
space shuttle 19
Sputnik 18
stagecoach 8
steam cars 14
steam trains 12
steam wagons 6-7

TGV 13
traction engine 6

Viking longships 4
Vostok 1 18